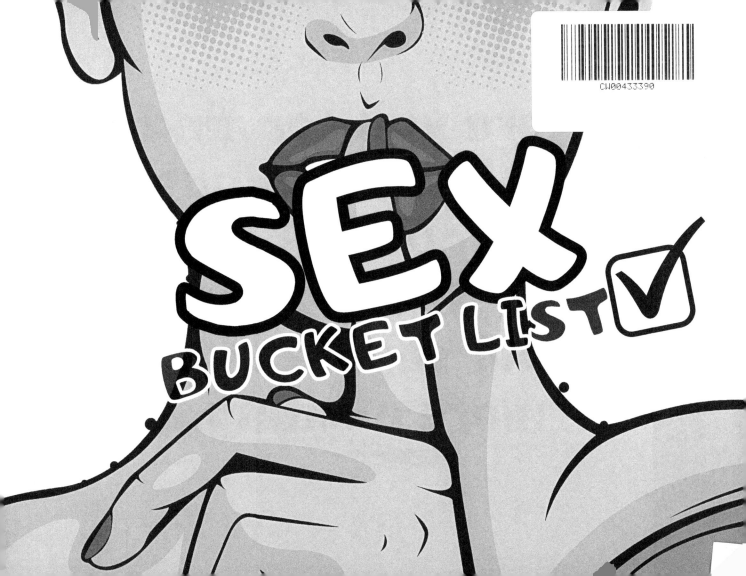

Here you can find 50 ideas of what you can do together to make your sexlife even more exciting.

PLACES
to have sex
before you die

A parking lot.

#2

A boat.

#3

A park.

#4

A top of a snow-capped mountain

#5

An old cinema.

#6

An office.

#7

A rooftop.

#8

A taxicab.

#9

A hotelroom.

#10

A restaurant or a bar toilet.

PLACES
in home to have
sex before you die

#11

A kitchen table.

#12

Under the shower/ in the hot tub.

#13

In a backyard.

#14

A stairway.

#15

In you
kids/parents bed.

#16

On the washing machine.

#17

On the floor.

On the chair.

Against the wall.

#20

A balcony.

SEX TOYS
to try before you die

#21

A blindfold.

#22

A bondage tape.

#23

A cock ring.

#24

A vibrating
panties.

#25

Collars and chokers.

#26

A finger vibrator.

#27

A dildo.

#28

Butt plugs.

#29

Anal beads.

#30

A sex Swing.

SEX TYPES

to try before you die

#31

Loud and
screaming sex.

#32

Silent sex.

#33

Phone sex/
webcam sex.

#34

Anal sex.

#35

Blowjob/ handjob.

#36

Sex while in costume.

#37

Ass fingering.

#38

A footjob.

#39

A threesome.

#40

A roleplaying.

SEX GAMES
to try before you die

#41

A strip poker.

#42

Sexy trut or dare.

#43

Sexy would you rather.

#44

A strip twister.

#45

Sex dice.

#46

Read sexy stories to each other.

#47

Strip-pong.

#48

Dirtytalking.

#49

Sexy cards.

#50

Intimate bingo.

Printed in Great Britain
by Amazon